The Black Crayon
COLORING AND ACTIVITY BOOK

Written and Illustrated
by Erinn Sneed

When I Grow Up
PUBLISHING

Cleveland, Ohio

ISBN-13:   978-0-9795117-6-9
ISBN-10:   0-9795117-6-3

Special thanks to:
Betty Sneed, Lavonda Talbert, Anita Rose Banks, Steven E. Boyd, Danny Queen, Ishmail Douglas, Darrell Bey, Wayne Chandler (author of "Ancient Future"), Harvey Zay, Steven Howard, Sharlyn Howard, Elizabeth Taylor, Andre Taylor (author of "You Can Still Win"), Michelle "Fenyx" Jackson, Jeff Phelps, John Phelps, Ronnie Duncan, Elisha Patterson, David Price, RaShimba Bloom

2nd Edition

In our family, Kwanzaa principles are practiced every day.

"Read and study! Knowledge is power."

The Jump

A Kente Cloth design.

I know myself because I know my history. Many scientists believe that all the people of the planet may have descended from a black female in Africa.

Ankh, an Egyptian African symbol meaning, "Life."

AFRICAN WORD SEARCH

This puzzle contains the names of 24 of Africa's 52 nations. Search forward, backward, up, down, sideways and diagonally. Once you find the word, circle it in the puzzle and cross it off the list.

```
T W M A L I J G E G Y P T J T C
A W Y E S H G H Z A I R E J R O
N I G E R T T A D K Y O U C A N
Z N B I L K U N P G E V O L I G
A N A Z I M B A B W E N C A N O
N E O E S A L G E R I A Y Z I G
I R U A Y T A H O M E I O A V P
A T B B I L I B E R I A M R A P
D A I Y O U L S A F E W N C A L
N L C A R E A N G O L A I P U T
A S M A R T M L O V E R A F O S
G H A T P Y O M O M F I I D E A
U I Y W E S S P Y A B T L N T O
P G A C E S Q E H I U M E I H C
O S U D A N S T M A C G O K I Y
G N I L U V U A E E A I K R O R
O O U O R O N B Y L I V E U P O
T W O U S O P W E A Q E P U I V
B O T S W A N A I B E N I N A I
```

1. Algeria
2. Angola
3. Benin
4. Botswana
5. Congo
6. Egypt
7. Ethiopia
8. Ghana
9. Ivory Coast
10. Kenya
11. Liberia
12. Libya
13. Mali
14. Namibia
15. Niger
16. Senegal
17. Somalia
18. South Africa
19. Sudan
20. Tanzania
21. Togo
22. Uganda
23. Zaire
24. Zimbabwe

Answers on page 32

11

My culture is on my mind all the time.

It is a beautiful day. I like to hang out and
enjoy the sun like my ancient ancestors
who built pyramids.

The queen that I am!

Color Flags by Number

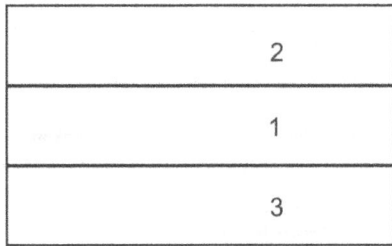

Black National Flag

color code
1 - black
2 - red
3 - green
4 - blue
5 - orange
6 - yellow
7 - purple
8 - white

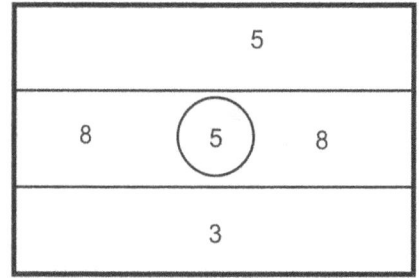

Niger

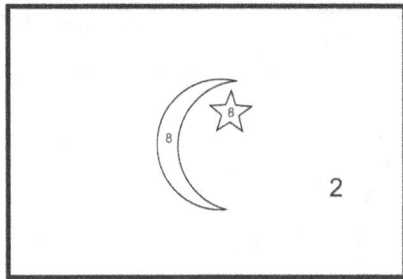

Moorish Flag

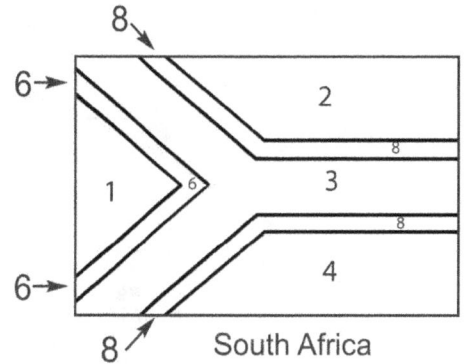

South Africa

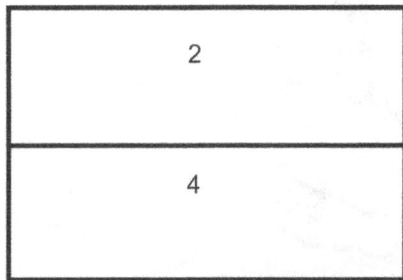

Haiti

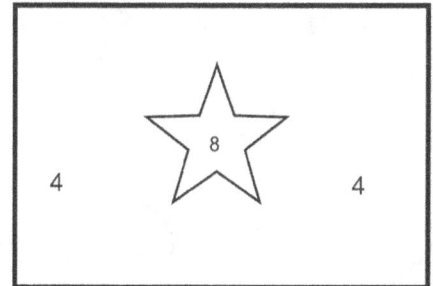

Somalia

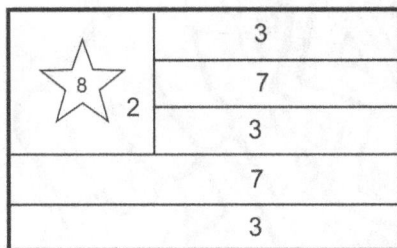

Togo

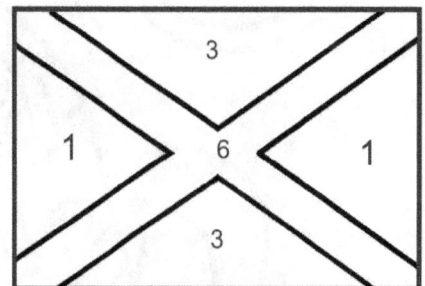

Jamaica

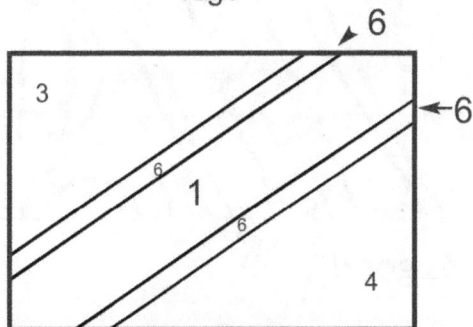

Tanzania

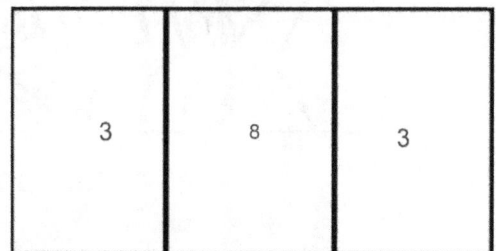

Nigeria

The company of a friend feels good.

Hidden Word Puzzle

```
S O U T H C A R O L I N A I G R O E G R Y W
A R M A R Y L A N D N E W M E X I C O Q N E
X H O H I O A R K A N S A S R T F F V O D S
E O R E G O N A T O K A D H T R O N R N A T
T D S J F P N E W J E R S E Y E T T E R W V
A E O C B K E N T U C K Y U H G H E I I A I
L I B M C O N N E C T I C U T C S Z S K D R
A S E N I L L I N O I S V H A S O C D J I G
B L R O A E G H G S A Q T R E N O E O M R I
A A I T M I O W A Y Y A O N A N L Y O I O N
M N H G O A T U R Q N L N I S A I N O M L I
A D S N H E S A R A I E V I W Y T N B W F A
I H P I A D H S I N T T N A J A K F B E A A
P B M H L F G S A N M A R H N F G V N Q J T
P S A S K D I K H C I E I A G I U I E M V O
I A H A O U S N A A H G T N H M A D W R E K
S S W W O A A T Z D W U R Y R M T A Y E R A
S N E L R G R E A E A A S I Y O G H O R M D
I A N B I B M D K W Q V I E V F F O R S O H
S K E H N J K P S E R R E I T S G I K I N T
S N C C O L O R A D O D D N F T F F L N T U
I I N D I A N A L U Y I R U O S S I M A S O
M I N N E S O T A U T A H G N I M O Y W C S
```

Find the 50 States of America

1. Alabama	19. Maine	37. Oregon	44. Utah
2. Alaska	20. Maryland	38. Pennsylvania	45. Vermont
3. Arizona	21. Massachusetts	39. Rhode Island	46. Virginia
4. Arkansas	22. Michigan	40. South Carolina	47. Washington
5. California	23. Minnesota	41. South Dakota	48. West Virginia
6. Colorado	24. Mississippi	42. Tennessee	49. Wisconsin
7. Connecticut	25. Missouri	43. Texas	50. Wyoming
8. Delaware	26. Montana		
9. Florida	27. Nebraska		
10. Georgia	28. Nevada		
11. Hawaii	29. New Hampshire		
12. Idaho	30. New Jersey		
13. Illinois	31. New Mexico		
14. Indiana	32. New York		
15. Iowa	33. North Carolina		
16. Kansas	34. North Dakota		
17. Kentucky	35. Ohio		
18. Louisiana	36. Oklahoma		

Answers on page 32

Drumming is a part of our heritage.

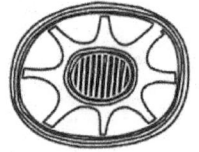

Sankofa

What Is Sankofa? Sankofa is an Akan symbol used in Ghana and the Ivory Coast of Africa. Sankofa means looking towards the past to create the future. This symbol shows the importance of knowing history to understand our present-day world.

There are eight Sankofa symbols in the picture above. Can you find them all?

Sankofa Symbols

Answers on page 32

I know that I am beautiful. A girl does not have to have long straight hair to be beautiful.

These masks were made by Africans for spiritual ceremonies.

When I study, a world of exciting possibilities opens up for me.

The cell phone was invented by Henry T. Sampson (a Black man), and was patented on July 6, 1971.

Black, proud and young; past, present and future king.

This is my home, the most beautiful house in the world to me.

KWANZAA
WORD SEARCH

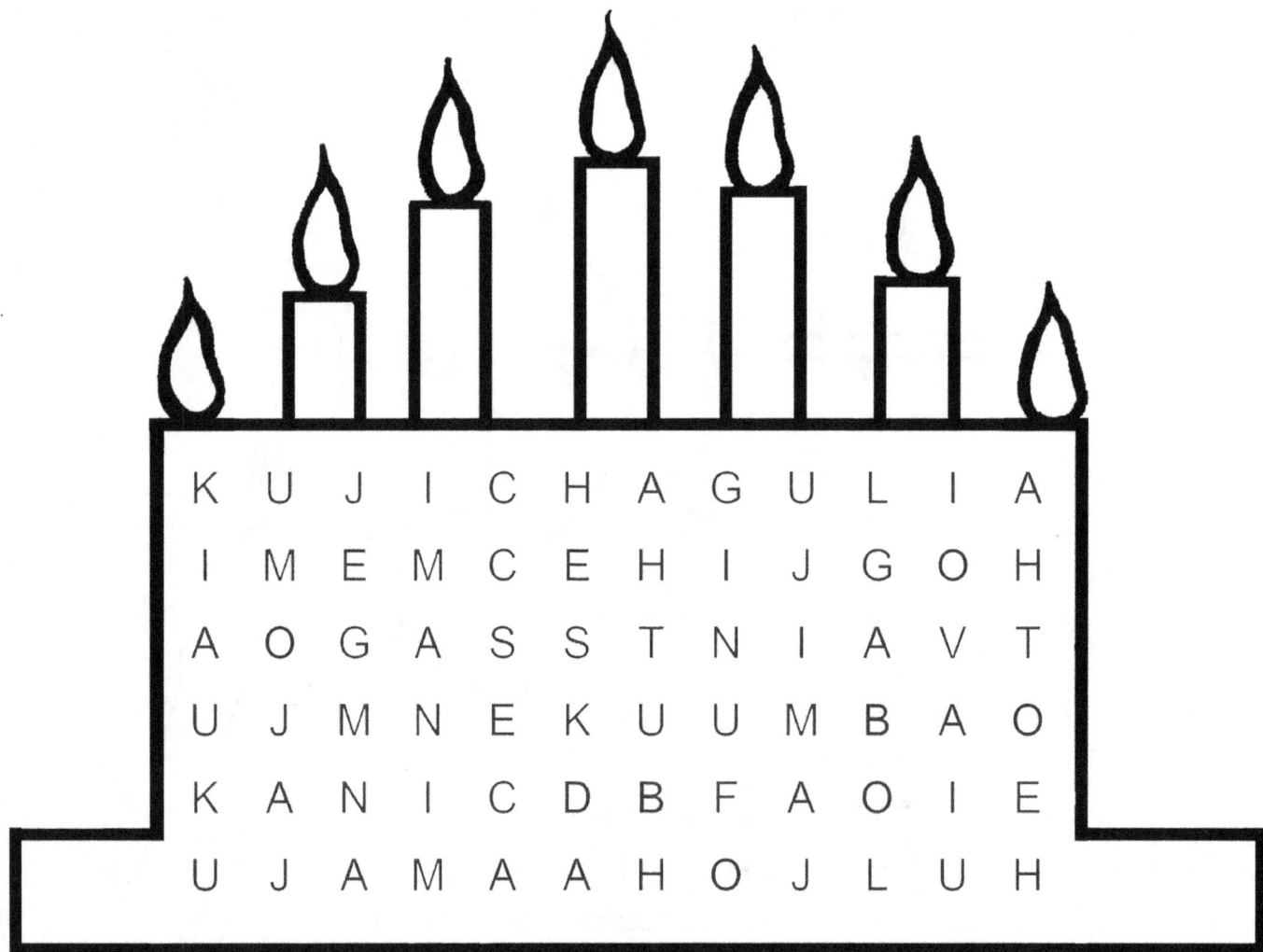

```
K U J I C H A G U L I A
I M E M C E H I J G O H
A O G A S S T N I A V T
U J M N E K U U M B A O
K A N I C D B F A O I E
U J A M A A H O J L U H
```

Find the seven principles of Kwanzaa hidden in this puzzle. Search across and down.

1. Umoja (unity)

2. Kujichagulia (self-determination)

3. Ujima (collective work and responsibility

4. Ujamaa (cooperative economics)

5. Nia (purpose)

6. Kuumba (creativity

7. Imani (faith)

26

Answers on page 32

Malik wears his hair in "locks" as an expression of his culture.

My brother and I love to go to the African American Museum to see the Egyptian art collection.

THE CLOCK OF
DESTINY

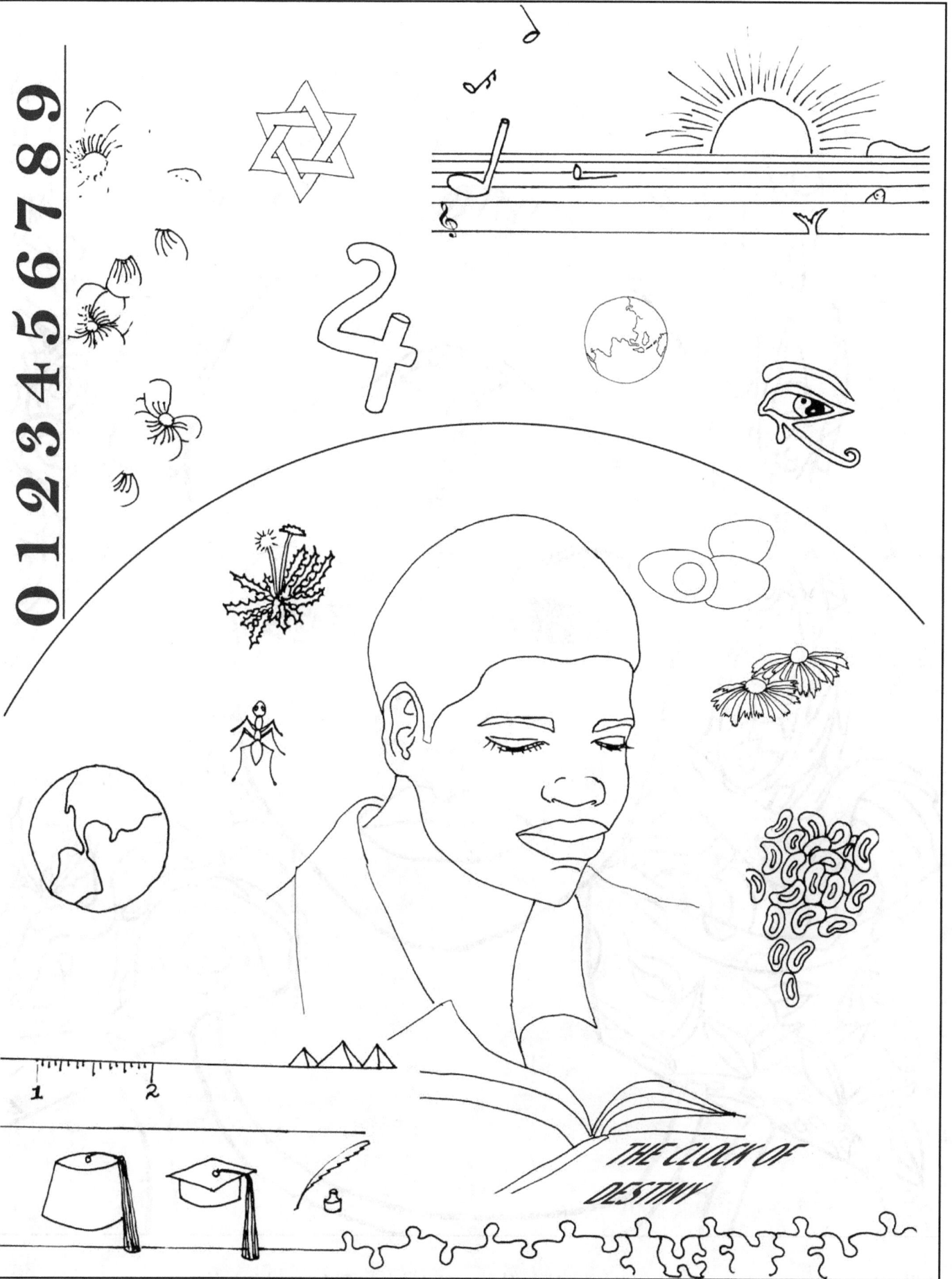

READ! It's in a book how black Moors ruled world!

29

I like to use my imagination. It's better than watching T.V., and it helps me to be creative.

Find the matching symbol

Each symbol on the left has a matching symbol in the box. Once you find a symbol in the box that matches a symbol on the left, draw a line between them.

Answers on page 32

Answer Key

African Word Search (from page 11)

Hidden Word Puzzle (from page 17)

Sankofa (from page 19)

Kwanzaa Word Search (from page 26)

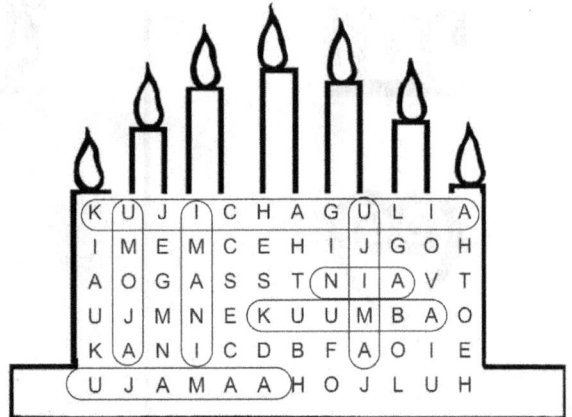

Find the matching symbol (from page 31)

Fun Notes

Fun Notes

Other books by Erinn Sneed

The Black Crayon
It's All About You
COLORING AND ACTIVITY BOOK
BOOK TWO

Written and Illustra...

The Black Crayon
A is for Africa
COLORING BOOK
ages 3 to 5

Written and Ill... Erinn Sneed

The Black Crayon
THE BIG CRAYON
Coloring and Activity Book
ages 3 to 5

WRITTEN AND ILLUSTRATED BY ERINN SNEED

vegan i am
COLORING BOOK
with Recipes
Activities and a
Resource Guide

Written and Illustrated by Erinn Sneed

Available on Amazon or email Erinn at erinn.sneed@yahoo.com

www.ingramcontent.com/pod-product-compliance
Lightning Source LLC
Chambersburg PA
CBHW081234020426
42331CB00012B/3168

9780979511769